How to TAME your THOUGHT MONSTER

HELP KIDS OVERCOME WORRY, STRESS, ANXIETY AND FEAR

DRAWINGS BY
Matthew McClain

ILLUSTRATIONS BY
Chuck McClain
Katie McClain
Allison Tannehill
Cameron Varnell

COVER AND BOOK DESIGN BY
Drai Bearwomyn

EDITED BY
Grace Kerina

FIRST EDITION
ISBN-13: 978-1484084175
ISBN-10: 1484084179
Printed in the USA

LEARN MORE AND CONTACT KATIE
www.katiemcclain.com
katie@katiemcclain.com

for

chuck

and

matthew

TABLE OF CONTENTS

WHY I WROTE THIS BOOK

AND

INTRODUCTION

When I was in my twenties, I began a great self-improvement project consisting of reading books, taking classes, and going to seminars. The list of things I did is long, and I did it all in an effort to feel better. I wanted to be happier. I wanted to find love. I wanted to get married and have kids. I wanted relationships that worked, that were fun and filled me up inside. All the time and money I spent were not wasted. I learned many useful tools and perspectives that have helped me a great deal in my life. The classes helped me meet my husband, and I incorporated much of what I learned into the coaching I've provided to others over the years.

In spite of all I'd learned, I found myself feeling stuck and unhappy after my son was born. I worried even when things were going great in my life. I struggled to find consistent happiness. I had love in my life, but I wasn't feeling much love toward myself. I was gaining weight as well. I referred to my earlier learning but couldn't seem to find what I needed in order to feel better.

Then one day, a few years ago, I took a weight-loss class with an amazing woman named Brooke Castillo. The class featured weight-loss tools Brooke had created for herself. Her tools had nothing to do with dieting, and they were different from anything I'd ever been exposed to. I enjoyed learning from Brooke, so I continued taking classes she offered. I soon learned about another tool she had created: Self Coaching 101. Slowly, as I started using her Self Coaching model, I gained new clarity and new insights and began to feel a whole lot better. Brooke's tool seemed to pull together much of what I'd learned over the years into a simple process that was very easy to use repeatedly.

The Self Coaching model is very simple – in only five steps you can start seeing the truth of your life, feel happier, and create success. In using this model, I not only gained the control I craved for improving my life but stopped stressing over things I mistakenly believed I could control. Now I use the Self Coaching model every day. I'm no longer at the mercy of my circumstances. I'm in touch with what I feel, and I create my life on purpose. The gold for me with the Self Coaching model was that I could do it anytime, anywhere, and it's been effective with every issue I've come across.

Basically, I fell in love with Self Coaching! So corny, but so true. I taught the process to my husband and my young son and was soon helping my family feel better and achieve the results they wanted, too. They began using Self Coaching to help themselves. I found that my son understood the concept much easier than I had. He creates success in areas that surprise me and my husband. Knowing our kids can overcome obstacles and help themselves in just about any situation is something all parents want for their kids.

I became such a fan of Self Coaching that I became a Certified Life Coach under Brooke's tutelage. As I studied and continued to practice using the model, I began to imagine what my life would've been like if I'd known about and used this tool in my preteen and teen years. I could have sidestepped so much struggle and angst. A dream developed of making the Self Coaching model accessible to children and their parents and teachers.

With the Self Coaching model, adults can overcome limiting beliefs and become the best role models possible for their kids. My hope is that adults use Self Coaching to reframe their own negative thoughts and to help the kids in their lives do that as well. Parents can model and actively teach this simple tool to improve their children's behavior and increase their happiness and success. Teachers can use Self Coaching to improve their own teaching and creativity and can also teach their students how to use the model – with the result of enjoying a happy and productive classroom. With those hopes in mind, I've created fun companion tools to use along with the Self Coaching model, to help adults learn the model quickly and to give them the ability to easily teach it to the kids in their lives.

Why did I call this book *How to Tame Your Thought Monster*? As you'll learn as you read, our thoughts play a huge part in our success (or lack of success) in life. We each think thousands of thoughts, many of which are generated automatically by what I call **Thought Monsters**. Though the thoughts generated by our mischievous Thought Monsters are mostly not very helpful, that doesn't mean we want to get rid of our Monsters. Squashing our Thought Monsters would only make things harder (as they say, resistance is futile). The idea is to tame our Thought Monsters so we can consciously create the life of our dreams.

In this book I'll show you each step of the Self Coaching model and present examples and activities you can do with your kids. I suggest reading through the book on your own first, to understand how Self Coaching works. Once you understand it and practice it yourself, you can go through the book with your kids and do the exercises together. You'll find tips to help you understand the model and to help with explaining the model's process to kids. I've written a companion guide for kids ages nine and up, which they can go through on their own. The title is *How to Tame Your Thought Monster: Kids' Guide*. You can find it on my website: http://katiemcclain.com/tameyourtmkidsguide/.

Once you understand the steps, I encourage you to complete all five parts of the Self Coaching model in order to see the results of your thinking. This will be especially beneficial to you and your older children (ages 13 and up). Younger kids may not have the patience for the complete model, but they'll likely be able to successfully use individual parts of the model to become happier and have more fun.

Once you begin to understand and realize the power of this tool, you can use Self Coaching to help yourself do all kinds of things, like lose weight, pay off debts, improve your relationships, and more. Your kids can use what they've learned to stop worrying about grades and friendships, and to create attainable goals for themselves.

Most of the children I've presented the Self Coaching model to seem to understand the basics and are able to use the tools by themselves very quickly. As a general guideline, I've found age nine to be a great age for starting to learn the Self Coaching process.

I'd love your feedback. Please feel free to email me to ask questions or to share your experience with using the Self Coaching model and teaching it to your children. My email address is katie@katiemcclain.com.

In the Thoughts chapter of this book, you'll get the opportunity to meet and draw your own Thought Monster. I'd love it if you'd send me a photo of your and your child's Thought Monster drawings. I'll be holding a contest: Show Us Your Thought Monster! (with prizes!). You can find out more and enter the contest by going to www.katiemcclain.com/thoughtmonstercontest.

For more information about Self Coaching, my coaching services, and classes that can help you gain a deeper understanding of Self Coaching, please visit my website at www.katiemcclain.com.

I hope you enjoy learning to tame your Thought Monster!

Let's get started!

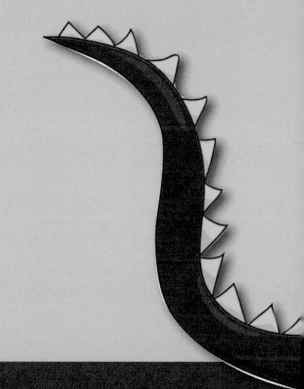

STORYTELLING

AND

HOW THIS PROCESS WORKS

Humans are natural storytellers. We each have a story about our childhood and our life up until now. We also have a story about our future. We have stories about the people in our lives, the events of our lives, and the good and bad times of our lives. Every one of us has stories about our lives, and each of our stories is unique.

If you asked two people who experienced the same event what they thought about it, you'd likely get two different stories. There might be only a slight difference in their stories, or the gap between one person's experience and the other's might be vast. We tend to cling to our own stories and hold them as facts. That's not a big deal unless the story we're hanging onto is painful. Our stories can take us out of our present reality and cause emotional pain, or they can lift us up and empower us to feel inspired.

Here's an example of how different people have different stories. When we were in our twenties, my older sister and I talked a lot about our childhood. At some point, I noticed that our stories veered off from each other and became different, even for events we both experienced. As we talked, we often disagreed about the parents we had. It wasn't exactly an uncomfortable disagreement, but it always surprised me. My sister's experience of our mom was very different from mine. My experience of our dad was very different from hers.

When I was a kid, my dad stocked shelves in a store similar to today's big-box stores. One day, he brought home some dolls and several outfits for them. I'm pretty sure he hadn't bought the dolls and clothes, since we didn't have a lot of money, so maybe he'd gotten them because they'd been damaged. The day he brought the dolls home, I was about seven and my sister was about nine. We were so excited to get toys on a day that wasn't Christmas!

My sister and I each remember that day differently. I remember Dad giving my sister the nicer doll because (as I told myself) he liked her better than me. When I tell my sister this part of my story, she thinks I'm off my rocker. She has a point. I have no factual evidence that my dad liked my sister better than me. So why did I think he did? At the time, I'd expected that (of course!) Dad would give me the best doll. When he didn't, I made up the story that he liked my sister better.

**Gaining awareness about our thinking is an important aspect of Self Coaching.
To begin gaining awareness, start by questioning your story.**

That day with the dolls, I was young and excited. My dad had a doll in each hand. Probably without thinking much about it, he just stuck out his hands, and the doll I wanted was closer to my sister. My seven-year-old brain *gave meaning to that fact*. In giving the doll I wanted to my sister, Dad must have liked her better than me. My many years of believing that story caused more and more pain for me. When we have a thought or story like this, our brains automatically go to work to prove it right. We start seeing evidence for the story everywhere. That's what happened to me with this story.

You may be thinking, "Well, but kids do that sort of thing all the time with their siblings and friends. I know the stories that come from it aren't true, but I know how to help my kids with it." Yes, you do, and that's great. But guess what? Adults also make up silly, unprovable, unhappy stories, just like seven-year-olds do. In fact, the stories adults make up and hold onto tend to be far more painful than the stories kids create. Kids can often change their stories in a flash. (That's why teaching Self Coaching to kids can make a world of difference!) Adults have stories they've believed for a long time. Adults have had more time to *collect evidence* to prove their negative stories true. That makes our stories harder (but not impossible) to release.

Until I unraveled it, my story about the dolls was a very painful belief. My father has passed away, but even if I could ask him if he liked my sister better, I wouldn't do it. If you're dealing with a similar situation, I suggest asking yourself a question like this: ***Is it true that Dad liked Sis better than me?*** When I ask this question of myself, I can't honestly answer yes. When I realized that continuing to believe that my father liked my sister better than me was a very painful belief to hang onto, I chose to change my story (more about this later).

Humans are story-making machines. We add meaning to everything. We do it unconsciously. Adding meaning to the stuff that happens to us in life is not necessarily a problem. It becomes a problem when we add meaning or make up stories that cause us emotional pain. We do this mostly unconsciously.

When we tell ourselves things like **Dad likes Sis better than me**, it causes emotional pain. We feel it in our bodies. When we make up stories that are negative, that have an unhappy meaning attached, we feel miserable. We don't want to feel misery and pain, so we start finding ways to avoid feeling those negative feelings. Some common ways we avoid feeling pain are overeating, drinking too much alcohol, working too much, using illegal drugs, overspending ... and many others. The irony is that the things we do to avoid our painful stories often end up reinforcing them.

My goal in this book is to show you how to find the unnecessary, untrue, painful stories you and your children are unconsciously creating. I'll teach you to question those painful stories and thoughts, and I'll show you how to change your negative stories and thoughts in a way that empowers you and makes you feel great. You'll get to start thinking about and creating your life intentionally.

You'll also see how you can stop letting everyday circumstances upset you. You'll learn techniques for allowing yourself to feel your feelings instead of avoiding them, and I'll show you how take powerful actions to create the life you want. This book is designed to help you learn the Self Coaching process and then teach it to your kids, so they, too, can learn to think on purpose and avoid unnecessary pain. Here's an overview of the Self Coaching 101 model:

THE SELF COACHING MODEL

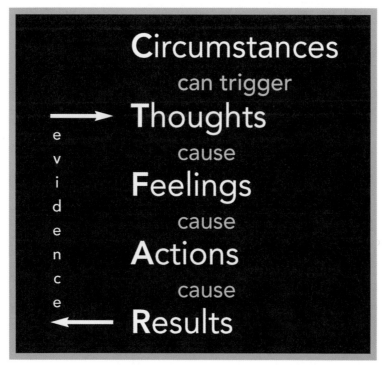

Circumstances
can trigger
→ Thoughts
cause
Feelings
cause
Actions
cause
← Results

evidence

©Brooke Castillo, Inc.

1   **CIRCUMSTANCES** are the everyday factual happenings, events, and experiences in our lives. Circumstances can trigger us to think thoughts.

2   We think **THOUGHTS** about circumstances, and this causes us to feel feelings.

3   **FEELINGS** are vibrations in our bodies. Feelings cause us to take action or not.

4   **ACTIONS**, in the context of this model, consist of doing something or not doing something. Actions cause our results in life.

5   Our **RESULTS** are the evidence that proves our thoughts and creates the current state of our lives.

The Self Coaching model was designed to be used in a linear fashion, with the five parts always explored in sequence, with **CIRCUMSTANCES** at the top and **RESULTS** at the bottom.

Below is an example of the Self Coaching model in action, using the example of the story of my dad and the dolls. Please note that even if you had a similar story, your model would likely look different from mine in this example. Your thought that created your story might be different than my thought, which would make your feelings, actions, and results different from mine.

CIRCUMSTANCE	Dad hands two dolls to Sis and me.
THOUGHT	Dad likes Sis better than me.
FEELING	Unloved.
ACTION	Attempt to be a perfect girl so Dad will like me.
RESULT	Unhappy.

The **CIRCUMSTANCE** is stated as just the facts. No drama or story here.

The **THOUGHT** is my belief about this particular circumstance.

The **FEELING** I state here is my best guess of the way I felt at age seven while thinking that particular thought.

The **ACTION** is also a best guess from that time. I likely acted out in other ways to try to get noticed by my dad. For some people, the above feeling might have caused them to withdraw instead of act out.

The **RESULT** of my thoughts, feelings, and actions in regard to this circumstance is unhappiness.

As expressed in this model, this is a pretty painful story. My guess is that you agree. I lived with the story that my dad liked my sister better than me for much longer than was necessary. Because I hung onto the story and didn't know to question it, *my brain unconsciously searched for evidence to prove that it was true.* As a little girl, I could have asked my dad if my thought was true, but I didn't grow up in a household where we asked those sorts of questions.

I present this example to show what kids do. No matter how happy your home is, no matter how open and loving you are with your kids, they will still make up painful stories and thoughts about things that happen. As soon as I learned about this model, I began teaching it to my son. He loves it and thinks I should teach it to every kid out there. (Yay! Here's the book!) But even with this knowledge, and even though he has loving and open parents, when we talk about his day or what he's thinking, my son sometimes still finds that there are painful stories he's created about the circumstances in his life. It's just what we humans do.

Later in the book, I'll give more examples for using the Self Coaching model. The examples can be very useful when learning about the model for yourself and for helping you teach your kids about the process. Sometimes I present partial examples of the model to show how the model builds on itself. Ultimately, and for best results, aim for practicing the model by using it as a whole.

In the remainder of the book, I'll break the Self Coaching model into its individual parts to help you and your kids learn how to use it. One thing I love about the Self Coaching model is that understanding and using a single part of the model can help shift your story. You may find that teaching even one part of the model to your child helps her start creating stories that empower her right away.

The Self Coaching process can help you and your children clean up your thinking so you think and create *intentionally*. When we become aware of and begin to clear out painful thoughts that don't serve us, our creativity soars. Suddenly, we imagine possibilities we couldn't see before! That's what has happened for me, my family, and my clients. I hope you find these wonderful tools simple to use in your everyday life.

USING THIS BOOK

This is a PLAYbook, not a WORKbook. It was created to encourage you to play with the material in order to learn, so you have fun growing with your children age 12 or younger. To present this material to teens, I suggest you let them read the book on their own, and I recommend that you share the videos my son and his friends created, which you can find at www.katiemcclain.com/tametmresources. You might find it handy to bookmark that link, as I've added lots of bonus content there related to this book to give you and your kids more learning materials for this process.

Each of the five parts of the Self Coaching model are covered in a separate chapter. Each of those chapters includes an explanation of that step of the model. Because each part of the model has its own unique character, I've created a **character tool** for each of the parts, to assist with understanding and solidifying the learning.

I've also included exercises you can do on your own or with your children. For maximum fun and togetherness, I encourage you to do them with your kids. The overviews and tips at the ends of the chapters offer additional information and add fun and inspiration.From here on, I'll often use initials for the five parts of the model:

C for **CIRCUMSTANCE**
T for **THOUGHT**
F for **FEELING**
A for **ACTION**
R for **RESULTS**

Though the Self Coaching model was designed to be used in a linear fashion, there are actually many ways to use it. There may be times when you want to address a particular feeling that's been bothering you, or change your actions directly. Starting with the chapter on **FEELINGS**, I'll show you ways to use the model to help you work through a feeling, or to start with a feeling you want and find a thought that helps keep that feeling present. I'll show you how to use the Self Coaching model to reach particular goals, take a certain type of action, or figure out why you can't seem to stop taking a certain type of action.

The first part of the Self Coaching model is **CIRCUMSTANCES**.

Here we go!

CIRCUMSTANCES

MODEL: PART ONE

Circumstances are the things that happen in our day-to-day lives. Circumstances are always facts. Circumstances can be proven in a court of law. Circumstances have no drama or feelings associated with them until we add the meaning.

Examples of circumstances:

C   Dad hands dolls to two sisters.
C   Child moves arm and drops toy on the floor.
C   Husband arrives home from work at 9:00 p.m.
C   Teacher keeps student in class during recess.
C   Friend walks away to play with another person.
C   It's raining outside.

We add meaning to a circumstance by thinking thoughts about the things that happen to us. We build stories about our lives through all the thoughts and meanings we add to circumstances. We can choose to create stories that feel good or stories that feel bad. Below are some thoughts that someone could think about each of the circumstances above:

T   Dad likes Sis more than me.
T   That child is a spoiled brat.
T   My husband doesn't care about me.
T   The teacher is mean.
T   My friend doesn't like me.
T   The rain is ruining my day.

Notice that all of those thoughts about the circumstances are not very positive. Some of them are blatantly negative. The fact that those thoughts are associated with those particular circumstances doesn't prove the thoughts are true. I could just as easily have chosen positive thoughts for the circumstances listed above. When you choose thoughts that feel good and that you believe for a circumstance, you're thinking intentionally.

WHEN CIRCUMSTANCES HURT

In some instances, circumstances physically hurt us. Examples of physical circumstances:

■   cold, fever, or illness of some kind
■   an injury, scrape, broken bone, etc.
■   cold or hot temperatures due to weather

Such circumstances are factual. Even for circumstances like these, people make up stories that cause emotional pain on top of the physical sensations they feel. An example would be someone complaining about the weather. Complaining about the weather is like complaining that leaves are green or water is wet. It's useless and can feel painful. You might as well choose a neutral or happy story about the weather.

QUESTIONS HELP TO IDENTIFY CIRCUMSTANCES

To practice noticing factual circumstances, remove feelings and judgments from both feel-good and feel-bad stories, leaving only the facts.

To help you find the stories in your day or your life, use one or more of the following questions and conversation starters. Then separate out the judgments, feelings, and drama from your stories to find the facts of what happened during your day. You'll notice that some of the questions automatically help you tell feel-good stories.

- What happened at school today?
- What did you do with your family today?
- What happened today that was fun?
- Tell me about your friends.
- What would you like to talk about?
- What happened today that made you feel good?
- What do you wish you could change about today?
- What do you wish was different in your life?
- What's going on in your life?
- Tell me about your family.
- What part of your day (or your life) do you want to talk about?

You can further help your child find their circumstances by using the info and play sheet pages coming up.

On the next page, you'll meet Charlie the Robot, the circumstances character tool.

"Think left and think right
and think low and
think high. Oh, the
THINKS you can think
up if only you try!"

Dr. Seuss

THIS IS CHARLIE THE ROBOT. I like the idea of using robots as a tool when it comes to the things that happen in our lives. Robots can't feel emotions. Robots don't make up stories. Robots see just facts. They see exactly and specifically what has happened. Things that happen don't make them sad or glad or scared. If there was a robot observing your life, it wouldn't get emotional about the things that happen in your day-to-day experiences.

Imagine you're a robot. You don't feel anything, not even hot, cold, or pain from an injury. If you were a robot, the weather wouldn't bother you. If you were a robot, you wouldn't make up stories. You would simply see clearly what happened, without judgment or drama.

Think about the last circumstance in your life that upset you. How would Charlie the Robot describe that same experience? Exactly what happened? Who was there? Were words spoken? Were there any movements made by the people involved? What else can you say about the circumstance that's factual?

The next time something happens that upsets you, think about Charlie the Robot. What would Charlie see in that circumstance?

I'll give you an example to help you understand how you can see just the facts of a particular life experience.

My son came home from school one day very upset that he hadn't gotten to take recess that day. He said he'd had to stay inside and do extra work. When I asked him why, he said his teacher was "mean."

This is how Charlie the Robot would describe the very same Circumstance:

> Matthew at school. All children except Matthew put paper in basket labeled "HOMEWORK." Matthew sits down in chair. Teacher speaks and points to words on whiteboard. Words on whiteboard read, "Please place your completed homework in the basket at beginning of class. If you do not turn in your homework, you will need to stay in at recess and complete it."

I knew my son's teacher well enough to know that there would only be a consequence like staying in at recess if there was a rule in place about it. When I explored the story with Matthew and asked him questions about it, he was able to see that his teacher was not mean. We also found that Matthew had created the story that he couldn't complete the particular type of homework he'd been assigned on time, and he was worried he would miss recess again.

So we created a new story. The new story was that we could figure out a plan to make sure his homework was done on time. This story included me reminding him in the mornings to put his work in the homework basket when he got to school.

Without the facts, I might have agreed that Matthew having to stay in to work during recess wasn't fair and that the teacher is mean.

Parents often do a great job of helping kids re-tell their stories. Charlie the Robot can also help, by showing kids just the facts. We may not always like the facts, but it's easier to tell a positive story and take empowering actions when we know the facts and look at them calmly. Looking for the facts of our own stories is a great way for us to alleviate our own suffering as well, helping us create stories and meanings about life that feel good.

EXERCISE
FOR THE ADULTS

FIND THE FACTS

Think about your day. List some of the circumstances that happened at home, at work, with your family and friends. Write out some of the circumstances as if Charlie the Robot had observed them. No drama, feelings, or stories should be included in your descriptions of what happened today. Try to write as if what happened is provable in a court of law. See page 13 for questions to help you find circumstances from your day.

C --

C --

C --

C --

C --

C --

C --

C --

C --

C --

C --

C --

C --

C --

C --

EXERCISE
FOR THE KIDS

FIND THE FACTS

Think about your day. List some of the circumstances that happened at home, at school, with your family and friends. Write out some of the circumstances as if Charlie the Robot had observed them. No drama, feelings, or stories should be included in your descriptions of what happened today. Try to write as if what happened is provable in a court of law. If you need help, ask Mom, Dad, or your teacher. See page 13 for questions to help you find circumstances from your day.

C _____

C _____

C _____

C _____

C _____

C _____

C _____

C _____

C _____

C _____

C _____

C _____

C _____

C _____

C _____

C _____

THINGS TO REMEMBER ABOUT CIRCUMSTANCES

Circumstances can't be changed – especially ones that have already happened. When we fight our circumstances by thinking negatively about what happened, we're basically arguing with reality.

Circumstances are facts that can be proven. Facts don't hurt. Circumstances don't need to hurt us emotionally. Circumstances are neutral (without emotion), factual, and without judgments that cannot be proven as true.

Here's an example of a circumstance (C):

C   I have a teacher.

When we add a judgment or emotion to a circumstance, it changes to a thought (T) that can't be proven as true.

T   I have a *mean* teacher.

The part of the above sentence that we can't prove is the word **mean**. One person's *mean* is sometimes another person's *nice*.

Our thoughts and judgments about our circumstances can make us feel bad, sad, angry, or happy. Our thoughts cause us to feel feelings. Feelings cause us to take an action or not. The actions we take (or don't take) cause the results we get in our lives.

**You get to choose the thoughts you think
about the circumstances that happen in your life.**

This is such great news! It means you can choose to powerfully create your life by thinking thoughts about your circumstances that feel good. It's really all up to you.

Many people think they have little choice about the way their life unfolds. Managing the stories you tell about the things that happen is a very powerful choice. What stories will you choose to tell?

HELPFUL HINTS

- Ask questions to help find the circumstance.
- The past is always a circumstance.
- The words should and shouldn't never belong with the facts.

TELL A BETTER STORY

When something happens that feels bad, you can use the steps below to practice telling a better story. You can use this simple process with your kids.

1 Tell the original story of what happened. Include all the feelings and drama.

2 Be a robot and find the facts.

3 Describe only the details of what actually happened.

4 Take out any words that are emotional or contain judgment.

5 Tell the original story again, with just the facts this time.

6 Finally, re-tell your story in a way that feels good or empowers you in some way.

Are you aware of the questions you ask yourself each day? Most of us ask ourselves questions all day long. We even wake up with a question. A common question I used to hear myself asking in the morning was

What is my problem?

When we ask questions in our minds, our brains automatically answer. If the question you ask is negative, you get a negative answer. When I started paying attention, I noticed that the answer I was getting to the question above was

I don't work hard enough. (A big fat lie!)

Not a very powerful answer, right? When I realized that, I started my days with a different question. You can choose to start your day with powerful questions. When you do, your brain will go to work answering with powerful thoughts, and that will help you create powerful stories throughout your day.

How do you know if you're asking a negative question? You'll know if the answer to your question feels bad. If you asked yourself this question from page 13 – **What happened today that made you feel good?** – you probably created at least one positive story from that question. However, that question is past-based. The questions in the feel-good list on the right, below, will help you with how your day goes today.

These feel-bad and feel-good questions show how questions can create positive feelings or negative feelings. They can help you teach this concept to your kids, and help you both get started with generating amazing days on purpose, by asking questions from the feel-good list. Try it out!

FEEL-BAD QUESTIONS

What's wrong with me?
Why am I so fat?
Why don't I have any money?
Why is parenting so hard?
Why is life so unfair?
Why won't my kids behave?
When will things get better?
Why do I make so many mistakes?
Why am I so dumb?
When will he start _____?
Why won't they _____?
What is my problem?
How long is _____ going to last?
Why aren't I more _____?

FEEL-GOOD QUESTIONS

What can I create today?
How do I want to feel?
What can I learn from this?
How is this perfect?
What's great about this?
How can I create what I want?
How can I figure out a solution?
What's funny about this?
How can I make today fun?
What do I love about being a parent?
What's great about my kids?
What's positive in my life?
What makes me happy?
What can I give today?
How is my body strong?
What's right about me?

THOUGHTS

MODEL: PART TWO

On the day you were born, *everything* was possible. I believe all humans are born positive, hard-working, and full of can-do spirit. If you've experienced the joy of watching a baby grow and develop, you probably know how amazing it is to observe them work to reach a milestone. Babies will attempt to roll over again and again until they get it. Then they'll continue to practice rolling over until that milestone is mastered. Not that the baby thinks of it as a milestone. It's just the next thing to do. The average baby instinctively knows what's next and works hard to get there.

Children learn quickly from their parents' facial expressions, words, and actions about when to continue, when to stop, and when something is a no-no. Our brains are like computers. Our brain's programming comes from our families, our culture, and the people we're around the most. We get messages from the people who raise us. We form beliefs based on the many messages communicated to us, and/or we hear actual thoughts spoken over and over by the people who raise us.

Here are some examples of messages that could be seen as negative programming:

- Finish everything on your plate.
- Money doesn't grow on trees.
- Success is difficult.
- Life is hard.
- Be a good girl.

These kinds of messages, combined with the thoughts we make up based on the circumstances we experience, contribute to our beliefs about ourselves, our lives, marriage, money, the planet, etc. Our brains get programmed and then automatically generate more thoughts based on that programming.

On average, we think about 60,000 thoughts per day. We also seek opinions from others, are bombarded daily by the media, and unconsciously receive messages from the people we work with, live with, and hang out with. This isn't necessarily a bad thing, but if we don't pay attention and remain aware of the painful thoughts our minds generate automatically, we can end up creating lives that don't make us happy and that we don't really want.

Research shows that when we practice and create powerful thoughts, we can actually change our brains and change the results in our lives. For a fascinating discussion on how thoughts and actions can change the brain, listen to or read this interview with Sharon Begley, the author of *Train Your Mind, Change Your Brain*: [www.npr.org/templates/story/story.php?storyId=7131130]

When we manage our thinking, anything is possible, just like on the day we were born. If we don't manage our thinking, magic and happiness are less of a sure thing. I've tried this idea out for myself. My life was already pretty good before I began noticing and managing my thoughts – it was by no means a pity party – and yet there were many days when I didn't recognize how good I had it and I complained a lot. Complaints are negative thoughts that we vocalize. I wasn't managing my thoughts, and as a result I often felt awful.

Now I create my life with intention. Since I began using Self Coaching, I've accomplished so many wonderful things, but truly the best part is that I'm happy most of the time. I can very quickly shift myself from feeling bad about something to feeling good. With Self Coaching, I appreciate and love my life no matter what's happening. Living from this perspective is an amazing way to create more of what I want in my life.

Helping kids manage their own thoughts is extremely useful. I'll give you an example to show how our thoughts can make us miserable and hold us back from life's experiences, and to show how you can help your kids think feel-better thoughts.

One of my young clients was worried and fretting about whether or not he would be able to handle a new experience he wanted to try. His thought was: **I'm worried about trying this.** Below is what his feel-bad model looked like, including the action and result he was getting with his thought:

Feel-Bad Model

C   New experience to try.
T   I'm worried about trying this.
F   Fear.
A   Obsessively think about the new experience. Stay home. Avoid friends.
R   Don't try the new experience. Unhappy. Lonely.

In our work together, we discussed how worrying isn't helpful for him or for anyone. Before changing his thought, we discussed whether he really wanted to try the new experience. We listed all his thoughts about it to help him get clear.

Sometimes, we really don't want to try particular things. If he'd been feeling pressure from his friends to try this new thing, his fear could have come from there. If that had been the case, we would've taken a different direction with his new thought, focusing on building confidence through honoring his own choices.

It turned out that my young client wanted very much to try the new thing, but was fearful because it was so completely new for him. We tried out several new thoughts. The one that worked for him is shown in this feel-good model:

Feel-Good Model

C   New experience to try.
T   I can handle this.
F   Confident.
A   Try out the new experience.
R   Fun. Excited about new accomplishment. More confident than ever.

My client did try the new experience. As a result, he had fun and got a big boost to his confidence. The new result proved his new thought.

24

Can you think of a similar example from your life or from your kid's life to plug into the above models?

Managing your thinking takes some practice, but you probably already do it in simple ways with your kids, good friends, and maybe even your spouse. It's likely that you already often help the people you love change their perspectives toward feeling better. Shifting our own perspectives is a bit like trying to notice the air we breathe, but the Self Coaching model makes it easy – and practice helps you get better and better at it.

Start by noticing your thoughts. Watch your thoughts the way a scientist observes an experiment. On my website, there's a meditation to help with this, which you can find here: www.katiemcclain.com/tametmresources.

On the next few pages, I explain what I call **Thought Monsters** and introduce an exercise designed to help you meet your own Thought Monster. It's a fun exercise to do with the whole family.

"A person who has good thoughts cannot ever be ugly. You can have a wonky nose and a crooked mouth and a double chin and stick-out teeth, but if you have good thoughts they will shine out of your face like sunbeams and you will always look lovely."

Roald Dahl

TOOL: THOUGHT MONSTER

ronaldo

We each have a little voice inside that criticizes us or sends us thoughts that hold us back when we go after an exciting dream. You may have heard this voice called a *Gremlin* or *Inner Critic*. I call it the *Thought Monster*.

There's a part of the brain near the base of the skull called the *amygdala*. It's a small lump the size of a walnut that hasn't changed much since prehistoric times. The amygdala, also called the *lizard brain*, is responsible for how we respond to fear. It's the part of your brain that triggers the fight-or-flight response. The amygdala and the ego make up what I call the *Thought Monster*.

Your Thought Monster is the voice inside that tries to discourage you from trying new things. It tells you when it thinks you didn't work hard enough, did a bad job, or look awful. Your Thought Monster often compares your skills and looks with the skills and looks of others, with you coming out on the losing end of the comparison. Your Thought Monster keeps you fearful and hinders you from reaching the goals you want to reach.

Your Thought Monster wants you to survive and to stay comfortable, so it doesn't want you to change too much, because that would be threatening. Your Thought Monster sends you thoughts like these:

- You'll never learn.
- They won't like you, so don't talk to them.
- Everyone will think you're weird.
- You need to be perfect.
- You're too fat.
- You can't do this.
- You make too many mistakes.

p squirelly

arabella

bloopy

We each have our own, unique version of a Thought Monster. Some are male, some are female, some have no gender and are just *things*. My Thought Monster is named Arabella. She's a tiny green lizard who dresses in bright pink and wears high heels. My husband's Thought Monster is Perfectionist Squirrelly. A client of mine's Thought Monster is called Bloopy. If this all just seems silly to you, it may help to remember that the Thought Monster is a metaphor, and metaphors can be very helpful.

Above is my son's Monster, Ronaldo. He's pretty cute, isn't he? That's because there's no need to be afraid of or mad at our Thought Monsters. After all, your Monster is just trying to help you by protecting you. The problem is that most of the thoughts our Monsters send us make us feel bad. Since your Thought Monster is operating from a place of fear (your lizard brain), the thoughts it sends out are not likely to feel very good.

Feeling bad often causes us to take no action or to take actions that don't help us. If you don't pay attention, your Thought Monster can create havoc in your life. Becoming aware of your Thought Monster is a great way to start recognizing the thoughts your brain generates that aren't helping you have the life you want.

Take a few minutes to think about the Monster who's sending you unkind or unhelpful thoughts. Notice the bad-feeling thoughts they send. Question those thoughts. Those negative thoughts aren't true. When you begin to question your negative thoughts and create new thoughts that you believe and that empower you, you'll be amazed at how happy you'll feel and at what good things you can create in your life.

MEET YOUR THOUGHT MONSTER

Have you heard the crummy thoughts your Monster sends you? Do you know what your Monster looks like? Does it have a name?

Meeting your Monster is a great way to start becoming aware of the negative thoughts that make you feel bad and keep you stopped in your tracks.

Here's how to meet your Thought Monster. It's pretty simple:

1   **Take a couple of deep breaths and get quiet for a minute.**

2   **Close your eyes and listen for him, her, or it.**

3   **Draw him, her, or it.**

If you don't want to or can't figure out how to draw your Thought Monster, try describing how it looks.

- Is it wearing anything?
- Does it have a particular job?
- Does it use tools or props?

Use the space on pages 28 and 29 (or your own paper) to draw or describe your and your kid's Thought Monsters. There are no right or wrong drawings or descriptions of your Thought Monster! It's yours and it's unique to you.

Thought Monsters may evolve. Though you don't need to ask your child to draw their Thought Monster more than once, if they love to draw, drawing their Thought Monster can be a fun exercise to do with them periodically. The bonus is the opportunity to revisit the idea of helping your kids stay aware of their unhelpful thoughts.

As my son Matthew has grown up, his Thought Monster has evolved and changed completely, as you can see below.

There's a fun craft activity you can use to bring Thought Monsters to life, one I've found to be lots of fun for little kids. Find out about it on the How to Tame Your Thought Monster resources page: www.katiemcclain.com/tametmresources

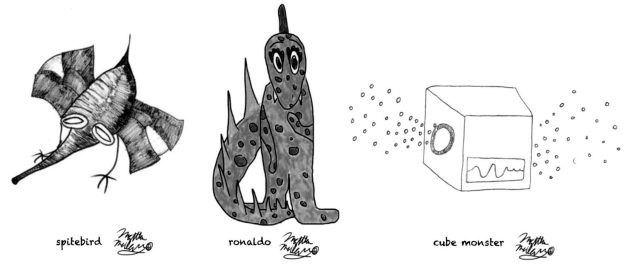

spitebird   ronaldo   cube monster

4 **Take another breath or two and listen for your Thought Monster's name.**

Just as there are no right or wrong drawings or descriptions of your Thought Monster, there are no right or wrong names. When I heard my Monster's name, Arabella, I was completely surprised. Yet that's the name I clearly heard when I listened for it.

5 **Spy on your Thought Monster to discover the unhelpful thoughts it sends you.**

Once you start noticing the unhelpful thoughts, you can ask the following questions:

- Is any part of this thought true?
- Do I believe this thought?
- How do I feel when I think this thought?
- Can I imagine someone else believing this thought?
- On a scale of 1-10, how important is this thought?
- How big is this thought? Can I make it smaller?
- Can I find anything funny about this thought?
- If my child was thinking this thought, what would I say to them?
- Is there any reason to keep this thought?

If you can, let go of the unhelpful thoughts. Later in this chapter, I'll tell you about changing those thoughts to feel-good thoughts.

Getting to know your Thought Monster may seem silly to adult readers, but that's only your Thought Monster talking. It may not want to be revealed. I've done this exercise with many adult clients, and they found it to be a very helpful way to start noticing thoughts.

If you'd like to hear me working with a client who's meeting her Thought Monster, check out the MP3 recording on the How to Tame Your Thought Monster resources page: www.katiemcclain.com/tametmresources.

Remember that without knowing our Monsters, we can't tame them.

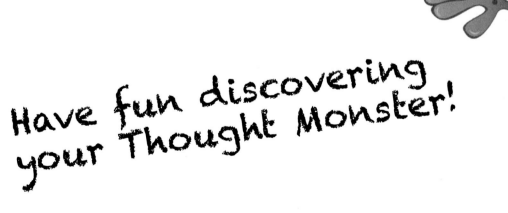

Have fun discovering your Thought Monster!

EXERCISE
FOR THE ADULTS | DRAW YOUR THOUGHT MONSTER

Do this exercise for yourself and for the kids in your life. Use the space below to draw or describe your Thought Monster, using the questions on page 26 for guidance. This is not a drawing contest, and your drawing doesn't have to be perfect. If you can't bring yourself to draw your Thought Monster, use this space to describe it. **Now get out some markers or crayons and have some fun!**

Be a spy and listen to your Thought Monster. What do you hear your Thought Monster say to you over and over again?

What feel-good thought can you think and believe about yourself, instead of listening to your Thought Monster?

EXERCISE
FOR THE KIDS | WHO IS YOUR THOUGHT MONSTER?

Get out your favorite markers or crayons and draw your Thought Monster below. Draw what you see in your imagination, but remember that no matter what your Thought Monster looks like, it isn't meant to be scary. After all, your Thought Monster only wants to help you, even though most of the time it doesn't do a very good job of it. **Have some fun now and meet your Thought Monster!**

Be a spy and listen to your Thought Monster. What do you hear your Thought Monster say to you over and over again?

What feel-good thought can you think and believe about yourself, instead of listening to your Thought Monster?

HOW TO CREATE FEEL-GOOD THOUGHTS

Meeting your Thought Monster is a way to help you start noticing your thoughts. That awareness is a great step. But you still need to do something about the painful, feel-bad thoughts you find. What can you do with those negative thoughts?

Here's how you can practice converting feel-bad thoughts to feel-good thoughts:

1 Write down your thoughts.

I suggest getting a journal or some paper and starting to download your thoughts by writing them out. Daily downloads are ideal. It's best not to leave those negative thoughts swirling around in your head. You can also stop and list your thoughts anytime you notice you're feeling bad about something. If you feel bad (and you aren't ill), ask yourself What am I thinking about right now?

It takes a bit of practice to notice thoughts, but keep at it and be patient with yourself. You'll get it. In the beginning, you may get frustrated or mad at yourself as you notice how many negative thoughts you think. Please be kind to yourself! Every one of us thinks negative thoughts – it's part of the human experience – so go easy on yourself. Focus on getting the thoughts out of your head so you can question them.

Young kids don't need to list their thoughts on paper. Downloading their thoughts verbally is all they need to do. To help your kids identify their thoughts, you can simply ask them to tell you what they're thinking when they're feeling upset. Ask them what's bothering them or making them feel bad (if they're ill, there's no need to do this). Usually, when kids tell their story aloud, you'll hear the thoughts that are painful.

As your kids get older (into the teen years) and are more private and cautious about sharing their thoughts with you, it's a great idea to buy them their own journal and suggest that they list their thoughts there. Let them know it can help to download their thoughts anytime they're upset about something or feeling bad, even if they don't know why they're feeling bad. Just like your skill of noticing your thoughts will improve with practice, theirs will, too.

2 Question your thoughts.

This step is very important! Thoughts are not the truth just because you think them. The thoughts that are true for you are the thoughts that empower you, that make you feel good, and that connect you to feelings of love and acceptance – especially love for and acceptance of yourself. This idea may be a new one for you. I encourage you to try it on and see if it fits.

Think about something in your life that makes you feel bad. Here's an old thought of mine that I had when I thought about being a mom:

I make too many mistakes.

I used to think that thought often. Then I questioned it.

Byron Katie has a process for questioning thoughts that I use often. It starts with asking this question about the thought:

MODEL: PART 2 - THOUGHTS

Is it true? You can also ask, Is any part of this true?

When I asked this of my thought about making too many mistakes, my answer was yes. I really believed I made too many mistakes. If you answer yes to the first question, ask this second question:

Can I absolutely know that it's true?

Answering this question was trickier for me. I honestly couldn't absolutely know it to be true that I make too many mistakes.

When I can no longer answer yes to Byron Katie's questions, I stop asking them and move on to changing my thought using the Self Coaching model. (If you'd like to learn more about Katie Byron's process, called The Work, visit her website at www.thework.com/thework.php.)

Try this with a negative thought: Think your thought and check in with your body to see how it feels. If it feels bad, question it: Is it true? If the answer is yes, ask this: Can I absolutely know that it's true? Unless you have a very strong and painful belief system around your thought, you'll probably answer no to the second question. (If you do have a very strong belief system, you may want to consider working with a coach to help you dissolve the painful beliefs so you can feel better and move forward.)

3 **Change your thoughts.**

If you can answer no to the questions above, you can choose to let go of that thought and look for a new one to replace it. Many thoughts are easy to just let go of. I encourage you to find feel-better thoughts that you believe to replace feel-bad thoughts. Believing the new thought is very important.

You must believe the new thought you create for yourself – otherwise, this process won't work!

When I looked for a feel-better thought to replace my thought about making too many mistakes, this is what I came up with:

The mistakes I make help me learn to be a better mom.

I believe this thought, and it feels much better than the original thought. This new thought is true for me. Interestingly, the new thought helps me see how false the feel-bad thought was.

Below are the Self Coaching models for both my old and new thoughts about making mistakes. I show the new feeling that the new thought creates for me (more about feelings in the next chapter):

Feel-Bad Model

C Being a mom.
T I make too many mistakes.
F Discouraged.

Feel-Good Model

C Being a mom.
T The mistakes I make help me learn to be a better mom.
F Encouraged.

THINGS TO REMEMBER ABOUT THOUGHTS

- Thoughts are triggered by the things that happen in our lives (circumstances).
- Many of our thoughts are generated automatically in our minds.
- Our automatic thoughts are the result of programming we received in childhood and interactions with the people we spend the most time with in the present.
- Become aware of your thinking by observing your thoughts like a scientist or by meeting your Thought Monster and spying on it to find your thoughts.
- Thoughts that feel bad are not necessarily true.
- Consider that the thoughts that feel good and empower you are the thoughts that are the truth for you.
- Choose to think thoughts intentionally that make you feel great and empower you to create an amazing life.
- The more feel-good thoughts you think, the more feel-good feelings and creations you'll have in your life.

Try using the thoughts below, or variations of them, as new, feel-better thoughts:

- I can do this.
- This was supposed to happen.
- This experience is what I need in order to learn.
- That's just _____ being _____ . (Insert person's name.)
- I can handle this.
- I can figure this out.
- I'm learning all the time.
- What they think about me is none of my business.
- I choose my thoughts.
- I'm smart.
- I'm happy.
- I love me.
- I connect with me.
- My child is acting exactly as they should be acting.

- This is the perfect response for a ___-year-old. (Insert a child's age.)
- All is well.
- This is happening for my highest good.
- This too shall pass.
- I belong to me.
- I belong here.
- I can be myself.
- I choose love.
- I am good enough.
- I don't need to make that purchase; I need to pay attention to me.
- This is perfect.
- He/she is doing their best.
- I create my life.

So, how do we find new thoughts that feel better? Here are some suggestions:

HOW TO FIND NEW THOUGHTS

- You can start by trying to turn the original negative thought around to its opposite (that's the process Byron Katie uses). Sometimes this works well and sometimes it doesn't.
- You can try adding the words **and that's okay** to the end of your original thought. Adding **and that's okay** can help you accept where you are and feel better.
- You can fiddle with the original thought, as I did in my example, to come up with an adjusted thought that feels better and that you believe.
- If the negative thought is about a particular person who is upsetting you, try thinking **That's just _____ being _____,** with that person's name in both of the blank spaces.
- Take the judgment out of the original thought. For example, **I make mistakes** is true and feels better than telling myself **I make <u>too many</u> mistakes.**
- If your thought has a **should** or **shouldn't** in it, switch the **shouldn't** to **should** and vice versa. Can you see how the new thought could be true? How does the new thought feel?
- Think about someone you admire, and imagine how they might shift a feel-bad thought toward a feel-better thought.
- Ask for help and suggestions from the people you care about. Try on their suggestions to see if they work for you. Sometimes, another person's feel-better thought can get you started on finding a thought that works for you.
- Try to find a brand new thought that you believe and that feels better. Be creative!

Thoughts are very personal. A thought that makes me feel better may not make you feel better. Keep trying new thoughts until you find one you believe. If you find a new thought that feels even a little bit better than the original thought, you're headed in the right direction.

In the next chapter, I'll discuss in more detail how to change thoughts to find better feelings.

USING THIS PROCESS WITH KIDS

When you use this process of creating feel-good thoughts with kids and you get to the third step on page 31, ask your kids for ideas about thoughts that would make them feel better. Kids are great at finding new, feel-better thoughts for themselves.

Don't be discouraged if a thought you suggest doesn't work for your kids. Remember that thoughts are very personal and that what works for you may not work for your kids. Encourage your kids to adjust the thoughts you suggest to them or to try different thoughts altogether. Try helping by adding **and that's okay** to their thoughts, to see if that feels better to them. Don't be surprised if the thought that feels better for them wouldn't work for you in a million years!

FEELINGS

MODEL: PART THREE

Feelings are simply vibrations or sensations that happen in the body. If you pay attention, you can get in touch with your body and describe how each vibration feels.

We often don't want to feel our feelings – especially negative feelings and really negative feelings, like shame. Of all the feelings out there, **shame** is the one most people try their hardest to avoid. It can even be hard hear or read the word shame. Do you know what shame feels like in your body? To me, shame feels like a punch to my chest. It took me a while to recognize that and to be able to describe the sensation.

You may be surprised to learn that intensely positive feelings are also difficult for many people to feel. When I was training to be a coach, I felt extremely happy. The learning was intense and the growth I experienced was pure joy for me. At the end of each class, I realized I didn't know what to do with myself – I was so ecstatic I couldn't handle the feeling. I'm so glad I kept doing the work I was doing, because it helped me become aware of what was happening. As I practiced sitting with my feelings and allowing them, I found that I could stay with the joy and that my feelings soon passed.

Our thoughts cause sensations or vibrations in our bodies. Below is a simple example to illustrate how this works with the Self Coaching model.

C The bedroom.
T There is a bed in this room.
F Neutral.

C The kitchen.
T There is a bed in this room.
F Confused.

Notice that with the first circumstance, the feeling is **neutral**, having almost no vibration. Most of us expect a bed in the bedroom, so this circumstance doesn't cause negative feelings. But with the second circumstance, the feeling is **confused**, which is a slightly lower-feeling vibration than neutral. A thought will cause a vibration depending on the circumstance that triggered the thought. (Also, it's possible that there's at least one person in the world who wouldn't be confused by a bed in the kitchen!)

The great news about feelings is that if you allow yourself to feel them, they pass in waves that last about 90 seconds. You can handle a 90-second wave of tears or a 90-second wave of joy. I promise. You won't die or explode! Many adults are so experienced at avoiding feelings that practicing experiencing their feelings is the only way they get better at feeling them.

This process takes time. Please be compassionate and loving with yourself as you practice it.

There are two kinds of emotional pain: clean pain and dirty pain. An example of feeling clean pain is suffering a loss, like when someone you love dies or you go through a divorce. You likely feel sad. You go through a grieving process. The pain of that loss, that clean pain, will lessen over time. Sometimes people push away their feelings of grief or think thoughts about their loss that end up extending the pain beyond what is necessary – that's dirty pain.

Here's a personal example of clean pain: My brother died in 2010. I still miss him, but I don't blame anyone for his death. I don't rail against the fact that he had cancer and died. I don't argue with reality and tell myself he "should" still be with us. I don't tell myself it's not fair and he died too young. I could easily do those things, but that would only prolong my pain and keep me stuck. Instead, I've allowed myself time to grieve my loss, and now I choose to think loving thoughts about him. I think of him often and remember all the happy times we had.

Here are two models to illustrate this example:

How I could feel

C   Brother died.
T   He was too young.
F   Angry.
A   Cry, rant about the unfairness of it all.
R   Angry, unhappy, stuck.

How I actually feel

C   Brother died.
T   I love him.
F   Love.
A   Remember fun, happy times together.
R   Loving my brother, not stuck in grief.

If you're feeling bad but you aren't sick or hurt and you haven't suffered a recent loss, then you're thinking a thought that's causing dirty pain. Negative feelings are your clue that your thoughts aren't empowering you. I'm talking about the average, everyday thoughts that make us feel uncomfortable, sad, left out, irritated, angry, annoyed, disconnected, etc. Sometimes we put on a brave face to avoid feelings, and sometimes we do things like eat, drink, or shop to avoid our feelings.

Ultimately, the reason we do anything in life is to feel good, to feel happy, but many people mistake avoiding bad feelings for feeling good. We believe that an absence of pain equals feeling good, but it really doesn't work that way. Continuing to avoid feeling pain only ends up creating a vicious cycle, one in which we never truly feel good.

Not every thought you have will cause pain, but if there are painful feelings associated with a thought or belief, first try to allow yourself to feel those feelings. The exercise on page 42 is designed to help you locate and describe feelings you may be trying to avoid.

Taking the time to use tools that support you in feeling through painful periods in your life is a very good thing to do. I'm not saying the process is *easy*, but it *is* worth it. In this section, I provide a tool and an exercise that can be helpful in allowing the pain and hurt you and your kids will likely encounter.

KIDS AND FEELINGS

As you probably know, the average kid is very good at feeling their feelings. They cry and express anger, sadness, and joy quite easily and frequently. At some point though, kids learn to control their feelings. The messages kids get from adults play a big part in what feelings they believe are okay to express. When our kids are small, we don't question the feelings they bring to us, but at some point we stop comforting them when they come to us with hurt feelings. Maybe it's because we believe they're too old for certain feelings or don't need comfort around some feelings anymore.

We all need comfort and acknowledgment; this can help us at any age. **We can give ourselves this comfort.** It starts with awareness of our thoughts and feelings. If your child came to you crying because a friend didn't play with her at school, you would probably listen to her and acknowledge her pain. You might allow her to cry and give her a hug before helping shift her story to something more empowering. I recommend that you do this not only with your children, but also with yourself.

USING THE SELF COACHING MODEL

Humans instinctively seem to resist negative feelings. If you want to stop having a negative feeling, you need to find the thought causing it, and then change it.

Let's say you're feeling bored. Ask yourself **Why am I feeling bored?** and apply the Self Coaching model. Here's an example:

C My day.
C There's nothing fun to do.
C Bored.
C Sit around, watch TV.
C Not doing anything fun. Bored.

Now let's look at changing the thought and creating something fun. One way to do that is to find a feeling you may be avoiding. Try to notice the times when you do something you don't want to do – like reaching for a cookie when you aren't actually hungry or turning on the TV when you have a million things to do.

Let's use the TV example to create a model. Ask yourself **Why did I turn on the TV**? Then wait. Pause for as long as you can stand it and see what shows up in that space. Try to find the feeling and the thought. Here's an example of how a model of this might look:

C My day.
T I have so much to do and I don't know where to start.
F Overwhelmed.
A Watch TV.
R Wasting time. Nothing done on my list.

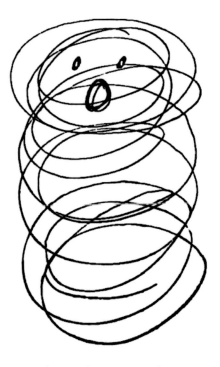

Once you find the thought that's causing your feeling, you can choose to change it. Here are new intentionally positive models for the two examples above, both with thoughts that create better feelings.

Unintentional negative model

C My day.
T There's nothing fun to do.
F Bored.
A Sit around, watch TV.
R Not doing anything fun. Bored.

lazy chaos monster

Intentional positive model

C My day.
T Let's find something fun to do.
F Energized.
A Play a game, go to the park, visit friends.
R Having fun today.

Unintentional negative model

C My day.
T I have so much to do that I don't know where to start.
F Overwhelmed.
A Watch TV.
R Wasting time. Nothing done on my list.

Intentional positive model

C My day.
T I can start by doing one item on my list.
F Certain.
A Do one thing on my list.
R Crossing items off my list. Progress.

Practice finding thoughts that feel positive, using examples from your own life. You can use the Find-Your-Feeling Ladder on page 40 and the instructions on page 40 as tools for naming your feelings or placing them in the negative, neutral, or positive range. On page 42 is an exercise to help you feel through your feelings until they pass or disappear.

"Whatever you do, you should do it with feeling."

Yogi Berra

USING THE FIND-YOUR-FEELING LADDER

The Find-Your-Feeling Ladder is a tool to help you access and label your feelings. It's a starting point for recognizing how your *thoughts* make you feel. Ideally, with practice, you'll get to the point where you can name and describe your feelings every time you need to examine a thought.

The circle in the middle of the Ladder represents neutral – feeling neither good nor bad. Above neutral are positive feelings, labeled as *Happy/Powerful Feelings.* Below neutral are negative feelings, labeled as *Sad/Weak Feelings.*

On the left you'll see a numbered scale that goes from +10 at the top, through 0 in the middle, down to -10 at the bottom. From 0 to +10 are good feelings. From 0 to -10 are negative feelings. Using this scale may make it easier to locate your feeling. If you're feeling positive or negative about a particular thought, you can find the number that best fits your feeling, remembering that 0 is neutral.

The Find-Your-Feeling Ladder includes some common feelings to get you started, but there are many more feeling words to choose from. You can find a more comprehensive list (in a downloadable PDF format) on Katie Byron's website about The Work: www.thework.com/downloads/worksheets/Emotions_List_Ltr.pdf (To download PDF files, you need a program like Adobe Reader. It's free. You can get it at http://get.adobe.com/reader/.)

Let's try finding a feeling. Think about someone you love. Get present with your thoughts about what you love most about them. Focus on the sensation that thought makes you experience in your body and ask yourself questions about it, like these:

- *Where is this sensation?*
- *Does it feel warm or cold?*
- *Does it have a color?*
- *What name would I give this feeling? Is this feeling named love, or do I have another name for it, like <u>adoration</u>?* (Feelings are very personal. Describe what this feeling feels like to you.)

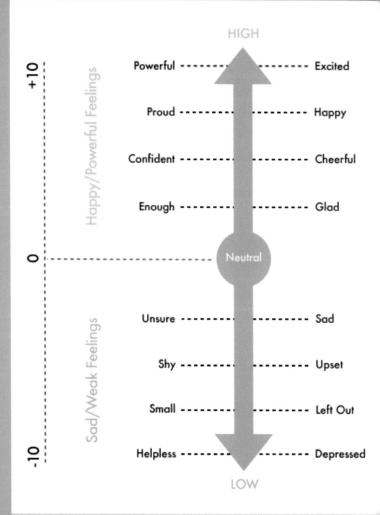

You can use the Find-Your-Feeling Ladder to improve your life. First, find a thought – think just one thought – then check in with your body and describe your feeling. You can then create a new *thought* that *feels* better. By finding thoughts that slowly move you up the Find-Your-Feeling Ladder, you can begin to change your life.

Here are the steps:

1 Locate your sensation on the Find-Your-Feeling Ladder.

2 Give your feeling a name. You can choose from the feelings named on the graphic of the Ladder here or from Katie Byron's list or use whatever name comes to you for your feeling.

3 Use the suggestions from the previous chapter on **THOUGHTS** to create a new thought that feels better to you.

Self Coaching newbies may have trouble moving from a thought that feels depressing to a thought that feels ecstatic. It's not impossible to do, but you'll have much more success if you find new thoughts that move you up the Find-Your-Feeling Ladder in small steps.

Here are a couple of examples of moving up the Find-Your-Feeling Ladder:

Ordinary feeling model

C I'm at a party.
T I don't know anyone here.
F Shy.
A Hide out.
R Don't meet anyone.

Improved feeling model (moving up the Ladder)

C I'm at a party.
T I'll be fine.
F Comfortable.
A Say hello. Talk to people.
R Meet new people.

Ordinary feeling model

C Today.
T It's just another day.
F Neutral.
A Ordinary effort throughout day.
R An okay day.

Improved feeling model (moving up the Ladder)

C Today.
T Today is a great day!
F Happy.
A Energetically create day.
R A really great day of happy experiences.

EXERCISE | FIND YOUR FEELINGS

Sometimes it's difficult to access and name our feelings. If you or your kids are struggling with this, try the exercise below. Move through the steps slowly, waiting for answers from yourself or allowing your child to find their answer before going on. Note that the words **feeling** and **sensation** are used interchangeably in this exercise. (For an example of how this process works, you can access an MP3 recording of me guiding a client through this process on the *How to Tame Your Thought Monster* resources page: www.katiemcclain.com/tametmresources.)

1 Sit or lie down in a comfortable position. If sitting, place your feet flat on the floor and your hands in a comfortable position.

2 Take two to three deep breaths. Pay attention to your inhales and your exhales.

3 Slowly scan up through your body, starting with your feet and stopping for a couple of seconds at each part of your body, moving all the way up through the top of your head.

4 As you move up, continue to breathe naturally and notice any sensations you feel.

5 Do you notice any tension, tightness, fullness, or other sensations in any parts of your body?

6 If so, where is the sensation located? What shape is it? How big is it? Does it have a color? Is it tingly, warm, cool, pressurized, hard, soft? Does the sensation move or change?

7 Continue describing the sensations as you scan your body.

8 Can you name the feeling of the sensation – like happy, sad, angry, scared, etc.? Try to be specific.

9 Ask the sensation why it's there? What message does it have for you?

10 Have you been resisting this feeling? If so, why?

11 Can you allow this feeling now?

Congratulations! You've just described and named what you're feeling!

Now look for the thought that's causing a particular feeling. Choose one of the sensations you've just identified and begin by asking yourself these questions:

- *Why do I think I feel this way?*
- *What experience or situation caused this feeling?*
- *What did I make the feeling mean?*

Now check back in with your body. Scan your body for the feeling that was there before. Is it still there? Has it changed? Has it moved? Is it the same color? Keep noticing and allowing the feeling until it disappears. Continue describing the feeling and asking questions about it in order to stay present with it.

If you stay with this process, the feeling will eventually disappear. Try it. Did the feeling disappear?

When you *allow* feelings instead of resisting them, they pass. Once a feeling disappears, you can decide whether or not you want to change the thought that caused it, choosing instead a new thought that feels better.

Remember that we can't change things that have happened (circumstances), but we can change what we *think* about those things. By doing that, we get to feel better.

In the beginning, it's easiest to practice moving up the Find-Your-Feeling Ladder a little bit at a time. Use the tips from pages 30 to 33 to help with finding a new thought.

FEELINGS

THINGS TO REMEMBER ABOUT FEELINGS

- All our feelings are caused by our thoughts (except feelings caused by circumstances like being cold, hot, sick, injured, hungry, etc.).
- Emotions and feelings are vibrations or sensations in the body.
- If you feel negative in some way, you're thinking a thought that's causing the negative feeling.
- You can change how you feel by changing your thoughts.
- Everything we do or don't do has to do with a feeling we want to feel or to avoid.
- Practice thinking a thought and then finding the feeling in your body that's caused by that thought.
- When you allow your feelings, they quickly pass through you. When you resist your feelings, they get stronger.

HOW TO HELP YOUR KIDS WITH THEIR FEELINGS

- Let your kids see you expressing and processing your own feelings.
- Model the concept that feelings can pass when they're not resisted.
- Talk to your kids about feelings and encourage them to feel.
- Do the FEEL THE FEELING exercise on page 42 with your kids when they're stuck.

serpent monster

HOW DO YOU WANT TO FEEL?

How do you think your life would be different if you lived from feelings you chose and wanted to have instead of the feelings you currently have? You can start your day by choosing how you want to feel. Here's how:

1 Think about the feelings you feel most of the time.

2 List your top three usual feelings.

3 Why do you think you have those feelings so often?

4 What do you think those feelings say about your life?

5 Do you want to keep your top three feelings? Even if those feelings are pretty good, you have the option of choosing better feelings.

6 What would need to change in order for your top three feelings to improve?

7 How would you like to feel most of the time? What would you choose as your top three feelings?

8 For each of the three feelings you chose in question 7, find a thought that will cause you to feel that feeling. Make sure you believe the thought.

HERE'S AN EXAMPLE OF USING THIS PROCESS

If I want to feel **happy,** I can think **I love my life**!

Now you try it:

If I want to feel _____, I can think _____.

If I want to feel _____, I can think _____.

If I want to feel _____, I can think _____.

ACTIONS

MODEL: PART FOUR

By now, you've learned that circumstances don't have to make you miserable. We've talked about releasing thoughts that disempower you and creating thoughts that make you feel positive. You've also learned the importance of allowing yourself to feel your feelings. When you do, feelings pass quickly. When you resist your feelings, that keeps you stuck.

So you've got great thoughts and you're feeling good. What's next? How do you create a life you truly want? You take *action*. All the things we *do* in life are actions. In the Self Coaching model, we also look at non-action. Our results come from the actions we take ... or don't take.

Sitting in your house and feeling good is probably not going to help you reach your big dreams. You must *do* something. When your thoughts are clear and your feelings are positive, endless creativity and ideas are available for taking action.

What do you want? Do you want to lose weight? Do you want to run a marathon, eat healthier or be more productive? Would you like to help your child improve his grades? Do you want to help your kids stop fighting with each other? Would you like to help a child who's been in trouble for bullying?

My guess is that you've already taken powerful actions in your life. You've probably worked hard at some point to achieve something you really wanted, like becoming a parent or getting a college degree.

I'll give you an example from my own life of wanting something and taking action to achieve it.

At age nine, I asked my mom to teach me how to use a sewing machine. I immediately started creating and I didn't stop. In high school, I looked into becoming a fashion designer, but the college counselor lacked information and resources that might help me, so she sent me to an extracurricular class for runway modeling. I'm only a couple of inches taller than five feet, though, and modeling wasn't what I was looking for anyway. I really didn't have any idea how to get into the fashion industry (the Internet wasn't available back then). The adults I knew kept telling me to be a seamstress. That's a wonderful profession, but it wasn't what I wanted to do.

After high school, I took some traditional college courses and got a job working at a precious metals trading firm. But I also kept thinking about my dream of becoming a fashion designer. My thought was:

I'm going to be a fashion designer.

One day, a friend I worked with at the trading firm told me that her roommate was a fashion designer! As soon as I heard that, I wanted to know everything. I especially wanted to know how her friend had become a fashion designer. The answer was that she'd gone to a fashion design college that was a mere 20 minutes away from where I stood at the moment I learned about it!

The next day I went to that fashion design college and enrolled. I stayed at the trading firm part-time while I attended college. Within three years, I was traveling the world as a fashion designer and merchandiser.

Something important to know about dreams is that they are simply powerful, motivating *thoughts*. I achieved my dream because I believed my thoughts about it. It took a lot of actions to realize my dream, but by continuing to think thoughts that supported my dream and by taking those actions, I got there.

Three important elements were needed for me to become a fashion designer: my *thought*, my *feeling*, and my *actions*. My model looked like this:

C   My career.
T   I'm going to be a fashion designer. (I believed this 100 percent.)
F   Passion.
A   Complete a fashion design degree. Work in entry-level fashion jobs. Work in freelance design jobs. (Plus many more actions.)
R   Become a fashion designer.

When I had the original thought – ***I'm going to be a fashion designer*** – I had no idea how I would do that. I had no clue that design schools even existed! In addition to my belief in myself and my dream and my willingness to take action toward reaching my goal, there were a lot of not-really-coincidences that happened along the way to help me.

I don't believe that finding a job in a trading firm, then discovering that my closest friend at work had a roommate who was a fashion designer was a coincidence. Also, that firm had a very supportive policy for employees who wished to gain further higher education. You might think I was just lucky, but I used those lucky opportunities to reach my goal. In other words, I kept taking action.

There are, of course, many other actions I could have taken in order to become a fashion designer. The point of my example is that I took action based on my thoughts and feelings. Yes, there were days when I wavered and felt fearful – that's normal when pursuing a big dream – but I kept going back to my original thought, which kept me feeling passionate and kept me motivated to take action.

All of that happened before I knew anything about Self Coaching. I point this out so that you, too, can review your life and see how the successes in your life look when put into the Self Coaching model. I encourage you to find success examples from own your life and fill out the model forms so you can see how the Self Coaching process works. Here are some questions to get you started:

■   What actions did you take that helped you reach your goals and create the success you wanted?
■   Can you name the feelings that caused the actions you took as a result of the feeling?
■   Can you identify the thoughts you were thinking?

When I first learned the Self Coaching model and looked back on my life, I was amazed at what I'd created! I was also very inspired to see how I could use the model's simple process to continue creating and reaching my dreams. Here are some questions to get you started:

■   What type of actions do you take in your life?
■   Are they actions you want to take or are you settling for less than you want?
■   Is your life just okay, or is it amazing?
■   Are you inspired to act to create the life you want?

Lives that are only *okay* don't take much effort to maintain. Great lives and fulfilled dreams happen when you actively create your life.

We take powerful actions when we *feel* powerful. Feelings that are above neutral and on the positive side of the Find-Your-Feeling Ladder help us take the actions that move us toward our goals. Feelings at neutral only cause neutral or uninspired actions. Feelings that are negative either cause no action or actions that don't serve our positively dreamed-of goals.

If you're taking actions you don't want to take, try putting each of those actions into the **A** (for **action**) line of the Self Coaching model (you can use the blank model forms on page 64, or create and use your own model forms). Then, working backward, find the feeling that caused you to act that way. Then go back another step and find the *thought* that caused that feeling.

If you want to change your action, put the new action you want on the **A** line. Next, find the feeling that will inspire you to take that action, put in the **F** line. Then find a thought that causes that feeling. Put your new thought in the **T** line. Here are some examples of models of recent actions my thoughts inspired:

Feel-bad model

C My book.
T I don't know how to write this section.
F Resigned.
A Wait around for inspiration.
R Book is incomplete.

Feel-good model that got me to take action

C My book.
T I really love this book!
F Inspired.
A Sit at the desk, figure out sections, write.
R Book is progressing.

Take a look at some of the actions you are currently taking. See if you can find the thoughts and feelings that are inspiring you (or aren't). Put the action you don't want to take into the **A** line of a model and work backward to find the feeling you have when you take that action. Then look for the thought that causes your feeling.

Use the same process to find an action you do want to take. Find a *feeling* and *thought* that will inspire you to take the action you want.

You can change or improve your actions. You can reach your dreams.

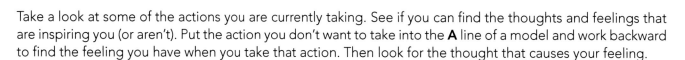

"Love begins at home, and it is not how much we do, but how much love we put in the action that we do."

Mother Teresa

CLAIM YOUR SUPER POWER!

Do you know that you have super powers? Your super powers are the things you do extremely well, things you do easily and naturally. You can spend hours and hours taking action with your super power and you'd barely get tired. My guess is you feel pretty good about your super powers.

Close your eyes and think about one thing you do really well. There are probably several things, but just think of one for now. You might think your super power is no big deal because it's so easy for you. You might be talented in an area where others aren't. Maybe your super power is so clear to you that you wonder why others don't love your super power as much as you do.

Action Annie is a super hero with many super powers, but her main power is noticing her thoughts. Annie's super power is called *self-awareness.* Because she notices her thoughts, Annie can figure out which thoughts make her feel powerful and which ones don't feel good and aren't helpful. She uses her super power of self-awareness to choose thoughts that feel great, which makes it easy for her to take powerful actions. By noticing and using her most powerful thoughts over and over, she's become a super hero in her own life!

You may not have been born with the power of self-awareness, but you can develop it as a power and be just like Action Annie. The more you notice your thoughts and the way they make you feel, the more of a hero you can become in your own life.

Let's use self-awareness to find the thoughts you think when you're taking action with the super power you came up with earlier. Think about the super power you identified. You have a natural ability in this particular area, and you also think super powerful thoughts when you use your ability. You may not have noticed the thoughts you think when you're using your natural super power. Let's find out now what they are.

Try to remember what you tell yourself right before you get busy being a super hero, whether it's with art or computers, raising kids, writing, playing sports, or doing your job.

One of my natural super powers is to share what I know. Here's a common thought I think and how it looks in the model:

C   Katie learns something.
T   I can't wait to share this new, exciting thing I learned!
F   Excited.
A   Make some notes, gather info. Share with whoever is willing to listen.

Once you find some of the thoughts you think when you're using your super power, try those same thoughts out in other areas where you want to take action like a super hero. You can use the same exact thought or you can try adjusting it slightly to help you feel a positive feeling that will cause you to take a powerful action. The exercise on the next page is designed to help you do this.

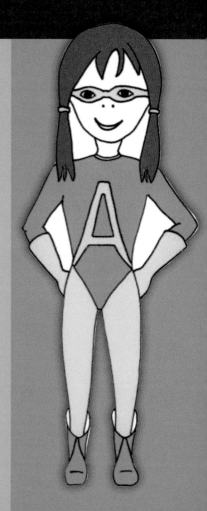

Annie is super aware of her thoughts. She notices the way her thoughts make her feel, and she chooses powerful thoughts that support her actions. Be a super hero in your own life by becoming super aware of your thoughts, too!

EXERCISE | THINKING LIKE A SUPER HERO

1 Put your name on the **C** line in the blank model below.
2 What's your natural talent? Pick one of your super powers and write it on the **A** line.
3 How do you feel right before you use your super power? Use the Find-Your-Feeling Ladder if you need help. Write your feeling on the **F** line.
4 Find the thought you think that causes the feeling you have before you act using your super power. Write your thought on the **T** line.

C _____

T _____

F _____

A _____

R _____

Here's my model, using my example from the previous page:

C Katie learns something.
T I can't wait to share this new exciting thing I learned!
F Excited.
A Make some notes, gather info. Share with whoever is willing to listen.
R Excitedly sharing what I've learned.

You can practice thinking like a super hero by following these steps:

1 On a new blank model (there's one on the next page), put your name on the C line.
2 What action would you like to take? Think of something you want to do but don't feel very motivated to do. Write the action you want to take on the A line.
3 Try out your thought from your super power model above in this new model. When you think your super power thought, does it give you a feeling that will cause you to take the action you want to take? If yes, write it on the T line.
4 Fill in the **F** line with the feeling you have when you think your super power thought.

If your exact super power thought doesn't work for you in the new model with the action you want to take, change or tweak it slightly to make it work. Ask yourself if you believe the super power thought in the new model. Play around with your old super power thought until it fits the new model.

C --
T --
F --
A --
R --

Here's an example of using my super power thought above tweaked a bit to fit the action I want to take:

C Katie wants to learn something.
T I can't wait to try this new, exciting thing I heard about.
F Excited.
A Schedule a session for indoor sky-diving.
R Have fun trying out a new experience.

You can use the blank sheet on page 52 to help you practice creating brand new thoughts that will help you practice thinking like a super hero.

spitebird

PRACTICE THINKING LIKE A SUPER HERO

(Start with **A** for the action you want to take.)

C _____
T _____
F _____
A _____
R _____

C _____
T _____
F _____
A _____
R _____

C _____
T _____
F _____
A _____
R _____

C _____
T _____
F _____
A _____
R _____

THINGS TO REMEMBER ABOUT ACTIONS

■ Actions are all the things you *do*.

■ Actions are powered by your feelings, which are caused by your thoughts.

■ In the Self Coaching model, both action and non-action are taken into consideration.

■ If your thoughts are not in alignment with your actions, you'll eventually stop taking action.

■ To reinforce a new thought, take actions that align with that thought.

■ If you want to change your actions, first change your thoughts.

■ To take actions you want to take, apply the powerful thinking that helps you with actions you're already good at.

■ Think about someone you know who takes actions you admire. Try out the thoughts you imagine they think to see if they help you take the action you want to take.

LOOKING AT BEHAVIORS YOU DON'T WANT

Do you have any habits or behaviors you want to change? If so, here are some questions that can help you shift your actions toward better results:

■ What do you feel prior to doing this behavior?

■ What is the thought you think prior to this behavior?

■ What is the result you get from this behavior?

■ Can you see how the results prove your thought?

These questions can help you change the behavior you don't want to something better:

■ What's the action you'd like to take?

■ How would you need to feel in order to take that action?

■ What thought would you need to think in order to feel the feeling that will cause you to take the action?

Here's another option for changing unwanted actions and behaviors:

1 Think of someone you admire who behaves the way you want to.

2 What do you imagine that person *thinks* before they behave that way?

3 Try that same thought for yourself, filling in the Self Coaching model.

THOUGHTS ON BULLYING

One of the biggest issues in our society today is bullying, which often has devastating results. A big reason I wrote this book is to help parents and teachers support the kids in their lives to be successful, happy, and contributing members of their communities. Addressing the issue of bullying through the Self Coaching model can help.

It's important to realize that bullying is an *action*. By examining their thoughts, kids who are being bullied can choose to be empowered and move forward instead of staying in the victim role.

Much attention is paid to children and teens who are bullied. We need to help and support these kids to heal. When recovering from a bullying incident, the tool of Self Coaching can help with locating the thoughts kids tell themselves. Kids can feel better by learning to question their thoughts about themselves, the incident, and whoever did the bullying.

Unfortunately, not much attention is paid to children who do the bullying. They're punished and ridiculed. What many people don't understand is that since bullying is an action and actions always begin with thoughts, it follows that if children resort to bullying behavior, they must be thinking some very negative feeling thoughts. Those negative thoughts likely begin with children believing hurtful things about themselves. That could be due to the child's circumstances at home or any number of experiences that have led the child to believe that something is wrong with them.

Children who bully carry beliefs about themselves that cause very painful feelings. Our thoughts stem from the ideas we have about how things should or shouldn't happen to us, for us, and around us. Negative beliefs build up. Children compare themselves to others. They start noticing children they think have lives and experiences that are better than theirs. They feel angry, hurt, or other very negative emotions, and the action they take is lashing out with words or force. The result is negative for the person who does the bullying as well as for the person who's bullied. This vicious cycle creates shame for all parties.

Shame is an emotion that almost no one wants to talk about, hear about, admit to having, or deal with. Adults aren't typically comfortable talking about experiences that were shaming to them, and this affects whether or not we discuss shame with our kids. Having feelings of shame is the reason so many bullied kids don't tell adults about their experience. When we're ashamed, we isolate ourselves.

WHAT CAN ADULTS DO TO HELP?

First, clean up your own thinking.
Use Self Coaching or another process to clean up and clear your own thinking on this topic.

Learn from Dr. Brené Brown.
Dr. Brown is a researcher who writes extensively on the topics of shame and vulnerability. She can help you understand shame and show you ways to discuss this emotion with your kids. In addition to reading her books, you can watch her TED talks and visit her website: www.brenebrown.com.

Listen to your children.
Make time to listen. Listen when your kids are in the back of the car or playing with friends. Listen when siblings talk or fight with each other. Pay attention to what your kids say. Listen harder. Listen more wisely.

Ask questions.
Ask your kids about their day and about their friends. Ask about the kids and adults at school. Ask what they thought and think about their experiences. Be *specific* with your questions. Don't interrupt when your kids answer. Listen and keep listening.

You can read my personal story about bullying by going to:

www.katiemcclain.com/the-truth-about-bullying.

RESULT'S

MODEL: PART FIVE

Results are the consequences, outcomes, and effects of your thoughts. Another way to say it is that results are the evidence or proof of what you're thinking.

To be honest, that idea was a bit upsetting to me at first. Did that mean I was to blame for the crummy results I had in my life? Yes and no. For a while, I did choose to blame myself for some of the results I had that I didn't want. But **blame** is not a very uplifting concept, so instead I chose the word **create**. Although my unconscious thinking created some of the bad stuff in my life, I also created great stuff with my thoughts.

Since your results are evidence or proof of your thinking, you can choose to see the evidence in your life simply as opportunities for teachable moments. There's no need to go to a negative place of blaming yourself. All you need to do is take a look at your thoughts and make adjustments.

What will looking at your results prompt you to choose?

In the opening chapter of this book (**Why I Wrote This Book**), I wrote about the extra pounds I was carrying when I first started working with Brooke Castillo. Those extra pounds were the results of my actions of eating too many sweets and not exercising enough. Why did I take those actions? One feeling that caused me to take those actions was boredom. I was bored because I thought and believed I had no purpose in life. When I put my *result* of extra weight in the Self Coaching model, it looked like this:

C   My life.
T   I have no purpose.
F   Bored.
A   Eat sweets. Watch TV.
R   Gain 20 extra pounds.

When I questioned the thought **I have no purpose**, I saw that it was a lie. My purpose at that time (and still today) is to be a great mom and to support my family. What was missing from my purpose was taking care of *myself* and managing my thinking. I knew deep down that I wanted to help others in addition to my family, but because I kept thinking **I have no purpose**, I couldn't help anyone else.

Those 20 pounds had things to teach me. I finally started paying attention. I took my first class and learned about the Self Coaching model. I took that first class to lose weight, but I learned so much more. At the time, I wasn't aware of the fact that my extra weight had created an opportunity to learn about myself, but it had. Now I know that every time I have a result that doesn't feel good, it's there to teach me something about myself. **This is such good news!**

When you have a result in your life that you don't want or that you want to improve, put it on the **R** line of the Self Coaching model and work backward to find your thought. What action are you taking that's giving you the result you don't want? What do you feel before you take that action? What are you thinking that's causing that feeling?

During my son's first quarter of middle school, there was a result he wanted to change regarding his grades. I'll show you how we used Self Coaching to help him change his result.

My son's first-quarter math grade in middle school was a C. That was very disappointing to him. If he didn't bring up his grade, he'd likely be moved to a lower math level the following semester. His dad and I didn't put pressure on him – we were more interested in making sure he was learning the concepts than achieving a particular grade – but my son really didn't want to move down a level, so we looked at how to bring about a different result.

First, we did some thought work together. We discovered that Matthew had brought his thoughts with him from elementary school into middle school. It became clear as we talked that his old thinking wouldn't cut it in middle school. He'd need to work harder than he was used to in math.

The result Matthew wanted was

 R   Remain in the current math level.

We learned that in order for him to stay in his current level, he would need to bring his grade up to a B by the end of the first semester. To help himself do this, he changed his thought to

 T   I'm willing to do whatever it takes to bring up my grade.

That thought felt good to him. He also believed it. (notice that this thought might not work for you or your kids)

We discussed what actions he'd need to take to bring up his grade. Since his dad is the math smarty in our house, we consulted with him, and also with my son's math teacher, to get ideas about actions Matthew could take.

The rest was up to Matthew. His new thought kept him motivated. He worked very hard, met with his teacher every week to get help with math concepts, and he double-checked his homework before turning it in. The result was that he received an A in math for the first semester!

Although I'm very proud of my son, I don't tell this story to brag. It was his goal that he worked on, not mine. We didn't push him, we supported him.

Below are the two models that helped Matthew achieve the results he wanted. In each model, we put his result on the **R** line first and then worked backward. In the first model, we worked backward to find his current thought. In the second model, we worked backward to find the thought he needed to achieve the new result.

C Matthew in math class.
T I am okay at math.
F Okay.
A Do homework quickly. Don't ask questions. Take tests without studying.
R Math grade = C.

C   Matthew in math class.

T   I'm willing to do whatever it takes to bring up my math grade.

F   Motivated.

A   Meet with teacher weekly. Take my time doing my homework and double-check it. Ask for help. Study for tests.

R   Remained in current math level! Math grade = A. Proud of myself.

I tell you this story to show how we get our results and how we can improve them. Your results always start with your thinking. Results are the evidence of your thinking. Your results prove your thoughts. You don't have to begin with an extremely negative feeling to work toward improved results. From any point on the Find-Your-Feeling Ladder, you can move upward, and in so doing improve your actions and, therefore, your results – just like my son did. With his new thought, his feeling changed from **Okay** to **Motivated**, both of which are feelings that are not below neutral on the Find-Your-Feeling Ladder.

"There is no such thing as failure. There are only results."

Tony Robbins

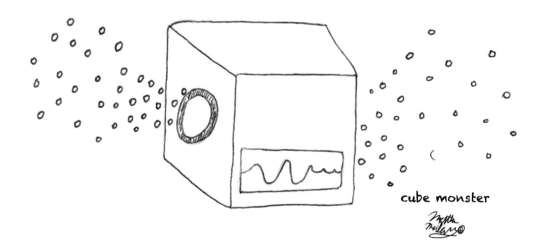

cube monster

TOOL: MAGICIAN

Using Self Coaching to create the results you want in life works like *magic*. It's magical to recognize that negative results are opportunities for learning about ourselves.

As I thought about what tool to create for this section, I realized that a magician would be perfect. *You* are the magician in your own life. *You* are the one who knows what you need and want. To create your own magic for achieving what you want, you only need to take a look at your thoughts, practice awareness, then, use your thoughts, feelings, and actions to help you create it.

In addition to the other Self Coaching tools in this book, I'm giving you a top hat and a magic wand to help you manifest your dreams!

As the magician of your life, you develop the skills for creating the results you want by practicing the Self Coaching model – first filling in the result you want and then working backward to find the thought you need to get that result.

I won't say that creating results is always easy, but the process is simple. With practice, you'll be transforming your life in no time. Some results you'll create will come sooner than others. Hopefully, those early results will motivate you to keep practicing your magician skills.

Use the blank model forms on pages 60 and 61, or model blanks you create to practice working your magic on yourself and helping your kids find their own magic.

Start by filling in a current result in your life and working the model backward to find the thought. Remember that the **C**, **T**, **F**, **A**, and **R** lines always stay in the same order, with **C** at the top and **R** at the bottom. It's also important to remember that all the lines in a model must relate to each other.

Here's your magic formula:

1. Write your current result on the **R** line of the model. You'll work your way up the model to complete it.
1. On the **A** line, write the actions you're taking that cause the result.
1. On the **F** line, write the feeling that's causing you to take those actions.
1. On the **T** line, write the thought that's causing the feeling.
1. On the **C** line, write the circumstance. Sometimes the circumstance is just you.

Below are a couple of examples. They were started by filling in the R line, then filling in the other lines, working from the bottom up:

Feel-bad result

C Arrive at work.

T I can't stand this job.

F Miserable.

A Drag myself to work. Do the minimum. Go home.

R Stuck and miserable in this job.

Feel-better result

C Arrive at work.

T Choose this job until I find a new one.

F Aware.

A Do my current job. Search for new jobs during breaks.

R Find a new job.

PRACTICE YOUR MAGIC

Model with a result I don't want or want to change

C --
T --
F --
A --
R --

Model with the result I want

C --
T --
F --
A --
R --

Model with a result I don't want or want to change

C --
T --
F --
A --
R --

Model with the result I want

C --
T --
F --
A --
R --

PRACTICE YOUR MAGIC

Model with a result I don't want or want to change

C ---

T ---

F ---

A ---

R ---

Model with the result I want

C ---

T ---

F ---

A ---

R ---

Model with a result I don't want or want to change

C ---

T ---

F ---

A ---

R ---

Model with the result I want

C ---

T ---

F ---

A ---

R ---

THINGS TO REMEMBER ABOUT RESULTS

- A result is something you cause through your thinking.
- Results are the effects of the actions you take, which are caused by your feelings, which are caused by your thoughts.
- If you don't manage your thoughts, your results will be hit-or-miss.
- If you have an unwanted result, use the Self Coaching model to find the thought that's causing the result, then change your thought to change the result.

A WAY TO CHANGE UNWANTED RESULTS

1 Make a list of the results in your life that you don't want.
2 Put each result through the Self Coaching model to find the action, feeling, and thought causing that result.
3 Try out the opposite of each thought. Fill in the model to find the feeling, action, and result you get with the new opposite thought.
4 See if any of those opposite thoughts gets you the result you want.

A WAY TO CREATE WHAT YOU WANT

- Make a list of what you want in various areas of your life, such as family, career, body, money, friendships, etc.
- Spend some time thinking about *why* you want what you want. Write it down.
- How will you feel when you get those results?
- Is there anything you can do *right now* to feel the feeling you'll have when you get the result you want?
- Using your list of wants, put each want on an **R** line on a blank model form.
- Working on only one result at a time, fill in the model backward. First, find the action you'd need to take to create that result, then fill in the feeling you'd need to feel in order to take that action, then fill in the thought you'd need to think to cause that feeling.

MORE QUESTIONS TO CONSIDER

- What result are you most proud of?
- Why are you proud of that result?
- What action did you take to cause that result?
- How did you feel when you took those actions?
- What were you thinking before you created that result?
- How can you use this experience and evidence in other areas where you'd like to change your results?

RESULTS AS EVIDENCE OF YOUR THINKING

When you find new, feel-better thoughts, the act of looking for evidence to prove your new thought is powerful.

An example is my son's new thought:

I'm going to do whatever it takes to improve my grade.

We could find evidence in other school areas that related to Matthew doing whatever it took. For example, he'd previously taken actions to overcome his fear of speaking in public. The successive baby steps he took helped him become increasingly comfortable with public speaking, so that by the time he gave his sixth-grade speech, he was ready. Getting over that fear required a big commitment, and because he'd been willing to do whatever it took to get there, that experience was helpful when he wanted to work on a model to improve his math grade.

PRACTICE USING THE MODEL

C = Circumstance, T = Thought, F = Feeling, A = Action, R = Result

Feel-Bad Model

C --

T --

F --

A --

R --

Feel-Good Model

C --

T --

F --

A --

R --

Feel-Bad Model

C --

T --

F --

A --

R --

Feel-Good Model

C --

T --

F --

A --

R --

SELF COACHING

THINGS TO REMEMBER ABOUT SELF COACHING

It's typical to make errors with the Self Coaching model in the beginning. I've listed some of the common issues here, along with how to avoid or work through them.

- You'll get the best results with filling in the models if you do it completely and correctly. Complete all five parts of the model. Practice using the model by starting with your circumstance and then completing the four parts below it until you feel comfortable using the model and consistently see how the results of your thinking prove and are evidence of your thoughts.
- Make sure your circumstance is completely factual. A common mistake made by beginners is to include or add feelings or judgments on the **C** line.
- If you've put a question on the **T** line, answer the question before filling in more of the model. Your answer is actually your thought, which should replace the question you had on that line.
- Beginners sometimes put in the wrong feeling in connection with a thought. Once you've identified your thought, sit with the thought for a few seconds or a minute to become aware of the actual feeling it causes in your body so you can identify it more clearly.
- Don't try to move too far up the Find-Your-Feeling Ladder too fast. It's much more effective to find thoughts that move you up the Find-Your-Feeling Ladder slowly.
- Check new thoughts by stopping to think the thought and seeing how it feels in your body. If the thought doesn't feel at least slightly better, it won't help you (or not for very long).
- You must always believe your new thoughts for them to lead to the results you want. If a thought feels better and yet you don't really believe it, it's not going to help you for long.
- Another common mistake is putting more than one thought on the **T** line. Here's an example of a thought you might initially consider to be a single thought, but which is actually two thoughts:

"My husband never does what I ask – he's so annoying."

Below are two options for models of these two thoughts. Notice that the action and result are slightly different:

C My husband.
T He never does what I ask.
F Annoyed.
A Avoid husband. Do it myself.
R Annoyed and stop asking husband for help.

C My husband.
T He is so annoying.
F Annoyed.
A Avoid husband.
R Annoyed and no connection with husband.

All the parts of the model should relate to each another. For example, in the models above, the actions and results relate to feeling annoyed with the husband and they also relate to the thoughts.

COACHING YOURSELF

You can use the Self Coaching process starting from any place in the model and working your way backward up the model. I've already given some examples of working through the model starting at various points other than the circumstance.

Here's another example:

Suppose you're feeling sad and want to find out why.

First, ask yourself, **Why? What's causing me to feel sad?**

You can write the questions in a journal and then write out the answers. Keep writing until you find the thoughts you're thinking that are causing the sad feeling. Often, this kind of inquiry can also help you feel the feeling. Use the exercises in the FEELING chapter if you need help.

When you've found the painful thought, fill in the model so you can see what actions you take with that thought, and the result you're getting. Then, when you're ready to change that thought, use the Self Coaching model steps, as described in this book, for finding new, feel-better thoughts.

You can complete the forms below to help you discover what you need to do, feel, and/or think in each instance.

If you're looking for a particular feeling:

If I want to feel _____, I can think _____

_____

_____

Complete the rest of the model to see your actions and results.

If you're looking for a particular action:

If I want to (do/be/have) _____, I need to feel

_____ and I would need to think _____

_____

_____

Complete the rest of the model to see your results.

If you're looking for a particular result:

If I want to have _____ as my result, I would need to (do/be/have)

_____, and that means I need to feel

_____, which means I need to think

_____

_____

A FINAL TIP

To practice relating all the parts of the model together, I recommend completing the circumstance portion of the model. However, as you improve your skill with using the Self Coaching model, you'll find that it isn't always necessary to add the circumstance.

A FINAL WISH FOR ALL MY READERS

C   Parents, kids, and teachers reading my book.
T   Self Coaching is simple and fun!
F   Inspired.
A   Learn and practice the Self Coaching model together.
R   Happy, collaborative families, teachers, and students whose dreams come true.

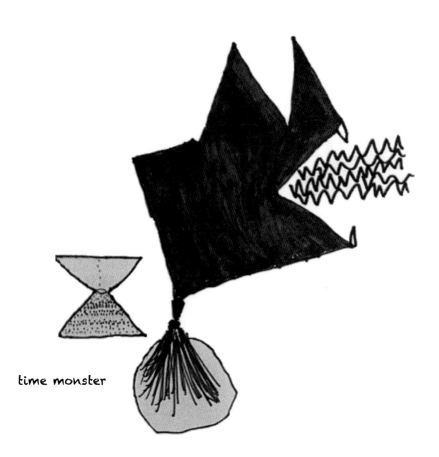

time monster

APPRECIATION

So many people believed in me when it came to creating this book. Often, coaches support their clients by believing in them before the client steps into believing in herself. Brooke Castillo did that for me, and it was a fundamental ingredient that helped me complete this book. I'm grateful to Brooke for teaching me her Self Coaching model and for empowering me to use her work to support parents, kids, and teachers.

The desire my clients and readers – past, present, and future – have to help themselves and the kids in their lives inspires me. I'm grateful they chose to read my words and/or work with me on their paths. A special thanks goes to Nichelle Jones and Allison Tannehill and her family for contributing to this project.

Thanks to Grace Kerina and Drai Bearwomyn for their brilliant and creative support in the creation and design of this little book.

Coaches are the most kind, supportive, and generous group of people I've ever met. Through their leadership, generosity, and support, these coaches have helped me move forward powerfully: Lin Eleoff, Laurie Foley, Melissa Foster Cook, Susan Hyatt, Michele Kittel, Suyin Nichols, Sarah Seidelmann, Jessica Steward and Sarah Yost. Thanks go also to all the Clear Coach girls I adore, especially my buddy Stacey Shanks, who's a very special and talented friend. I'm so grateful to the Rowdies and my Life Coach School group for all I've learned from and with them. They continue to inspire me daily.

My best friend, Linda Robson, who's loved me since I was 16, made me laugh and offered perspectives that always reaffirmed my sanity. Linda is the most inspiring woman I know. She's more like a sister than a friend and I'm blessed to share in this life with her.

I am so grateful for my family of McClains, Taylors and Hirigoyens, who are ultra supportive and who continue to teach me, and for my original family.

My son Matthew inspires me **EVERY SINGLE DAY.** He lights up my days and is my greatest teacher. I'm thankful that he patiently puts up with his share-a-saurus Mama and shows me what's possible for other kids. I'm continually amazed by him and love him **SO MUCH!**

My husband Chuck is the **BEST** man I've ever met. He enthusiastically supports my wacky ideas, believes in me unwaveringly, and never dismisses my brainstorms. I thank him for loving this book from the very first draft and for his editing and content suggestions. He helped me make the book lots better. I'm incredibly thankful for him and adore him.

Thank you for reading and sharing this book with the kids in your life!

For questions and more information, contact me via my website:

WWW.KATIEMCCLAIN.COM

Made in the USA
Monee, IL
03 February 2020